Old Times – Modern Times

A Different Breed

Edna Lambourne

Cover by

Published by Bite-Sized Books Ltd 2024

Bite-Sized Books Ltd 8th Floor, 20 St. Andrews Street, London EC4A 3AY, UK

Registered in the UK. Company Registration

No: 9395379

ISBN: 978-1-7385584-8-3

Dedication

for

My Family

Edna Lambourne aged 21

1. Beginning

So many people have recently asked me what it was like when I was young. It was so different ninety plus years ago that when I try to tell them they just don't believe me.

So I will start at the beginning.

Mr Abraham Cottrell bought a small cottage called *The Salt Box* in the 1900s. it was up a dirt track between Nuffield and Stoke Row, near Henley on Thames. Abraham and his wife moved in with their three month old son, William.

Abraham was a coppice worker, better known today as a *forestry worker*. He cut bean rods and pea sticks and sold logs for open fires, or, as most people had in those days, leaded ranges. These had to be cleaned every day as this was the only cooker people had. Abraham was also well known for making besom brooms.

In all, the family had a twenty two acre small holding, and Abraham kept pigs, cows, geese, chickens and ducks. There was also a very large garden where all kinds of vegetables were grown, plus Bramley apples, plum and damson trees, and also something called a *Bullus fruit tree.* This was a green fruit like the size of a damson. They were extremely sour fruit, but Mrs Edith Mary Cottrell found they were wonderful for wine-making.

Their nearest neighbours were across a field. One was a Mrs Wickson who had about five children, and they lived in a green bungalow. The other neighbours were a Mr and Mrs Tubb, who were quite elderly and lived across a different field.

Mr and Mrs Cottrell had five children and the youngest, born on 12th May 1933, they named Edna May Ann and that is me. All the children were Christened at Stoke Row Church in Stoke Row.

When it came to William starting school at age five, Mr and Mrs Cottrell were told that he had to go to Nuffield Primary School, which was a two mile walk. All the children went to Nuffield Primary, but even if we had all gone to Stoke Row School it would still have been a two miles walk. We had to take packed lunches. I remember that we had a small bottle of milk every day at school.

We were taught how to clean our own shoes every night and to clean the backs of the shoes as these were often missed by the cleaner.

We had no running water, only two very deep wells, one at the corner of the house, the other in the field for the cattle.

We had no electricity. All we had was an Aladdin Lamp put on the middle of the table. I must say the light from it was amazing but you had to make sure you cleaned the wick quite often, otherwise the light wasn't so good and it smoked a bit.

There were no telephones only a public phone box in every village. We didn't have a wireless, and papers were left in a box under a tree at the bottom of the lane.

I can only remember the wells running dry once – and then the Water Board people put a stand pipe at the bottom of the lane. My father managed to get a pair of yokes, which were a board across the shoulders, and chains on each side where you fixed a bucket. So much easier to carry that way with two bucket-fulls.

Our toilet was like all the others around the village. We had to walk up the garden to get to it. It was like a shed to look at from the outside. On opening the door there was a child size seat on the left hand side and on the right hand side there was an adult size seat. In my day it was called a privy.

We had two hurricane lamps – both for use outside. Dad had one to get the cows into their stalls from the field when it was dark. The other was used if anyone in the household wanted to go outside. They showed a beautiful bright light but once again the glass had to be kept clean.

We had extremely hot summers which I must say were always too hot for me. The winters were so cold with snow drifts five to six feet deep. Frost often used to creep inside the bedroom windows during the night, to be found in the morning.

Mum told me that Dad had to go to court once because he wouldn't send his children to school in very wet weather to sit in class in wet clothes. He won his case. He had had rheumatic fever twice when he was young, so I guess he made sure because of health reasons.

Mum used to buy toothpaste called Gibbs Toothpaste, which was a small, round, flat tin with pink paste inside. Only a small amount was needed.

By this time my second brother, John, had started school, and my sister, Ivy, would just have been starting school.

People from the villages and the neighbours were very kind. As most of the other children were older than we were, a number of bags were brought along to see if Mum could use any of it. Shoes were very difficult to buy new, as you could only get them from Reading town. This meant walking to Stoke Row to get the number seven bus, which stopped outside the shop and post office. A Mrs Gillett who owned it tried to get anything in the grocery line – the things people most needed – because it was only a very small shop.

I remember my Mum having what was called a *separator* which separated the milk from the cream. One day Dad brought a milk churn home from one of the markets he went to. A milk churn is a big wooden drum with a small round hole in the front, with a stopper. It had a top to it and a handle nestled in the wooden frame. The cream was put into the churn and the handle was turned for a while and when Mum could hear the different sound from the churn, the stopper was opened at the front. Into a bucket went the remaining liquid which was called *butter milk*. This was used to feed the pigs with their pig meal. What was left in the churn was pure fresh butter.

(I was taken back to my childhood a few months ago when I was watching *The Repair Shop.* Somebody brought a milk churn in to be repaired. After it was repaired, they made some butter and couldn't believe how good it was.)

Mum used to weigh the butter and sometimes make it into one pound[1] blocks.

We used to get very hot weather so the butter and milk used to be placed in a clean bucket with a clean tea cloth on top and then put down the well on a strong rope. This acted like a fridge would today.

Like most people in the villages around, we had a long tin bath. This was used once a week. Whatever containers could hold water and could be placed on top of the range to boil the water were used. Usually my sister and I were put in the bath together, once Mum had made sure the water was just the right temperature. While we were having our bath, Mum used to wash our long hair, which was plaited every day. No shampoo, just blocks of Red Lifebuoy soap.

---

[1] About 450 grammes

For washing sheets and clothes on Mondays, there was a wash house by the side of the house. In the corner was a copper, with a fire underneath. It took ages to boil because we had to make sure the fire was kept alight – and the wood burnt away so quickly. I can remember Sunlight soap flakes were added to the boiling water, once the sheets were already in the copper. Once boiled long enough, they were taken from the copper by what Mum called a *copper stick*. This was about twelve inches long and about an inch thick. It was a really dangerous thing to do, what with the fire underneath and taking double or single sheets out to be put into another bath for rinsing. Anything could have happened, but thank goodness it never did. In today's world, Health and Safety would have had something to say.

When it came to ironing the washed clothes, Mum had two flat irons which had to be heated on the range. We didn't have ironing boards as everyone used their kitchen tables, with a blanket and a sheet on top.

2. School

In those days children weren't allowed to start school before they were five years old. I couldn't wait to start but had to wait until the September term started. By now my big sister and youngest brother, Alfred, were in the junior class.

I loved school from the word go. I couldn't wait to learn. Mum had taught me a few letters.

When our teacher Mrs Biggs arrived, (she had also walked from Stoke Row Farm) we all had to stand in a line and wish her *Good Morning Miss.* Good discipline to start off with. We had 35 children in our class and 35 children in the junior class. I remember that first of all the new children had to learn their letters. We each had a reading book – one page had a picture of a cat: CAT; the next page a dog: DOG. Then we had to pronounce the letters. Once we had mastered that we were able to make sentences.

The next subject was times tables – from 1 to 12. Once we did that properly we had an exercise book with our names, age and class on the top. We were then set sums to do. When we were finished the teacher collected them all up. We had a small bottle of milk half way through the morning.

We had PE lessons every day, where a skipping rope was used to teach us to skip. We had to see how far we could jump. There was hopscotch, and the boys played marbles.

The nature walks were really enjoyable with the teacher telling us about changes in the trees at different seasons. I remember we went on a walk where the horse chestnut trees hadn't come into leaf. The teacher broke off a piece where there would be a leaf coming. She told us to touch the end of the stem and I remember it being very sticky. She said they are called *sticky buds.* We took it back to school and put it in a jam jar of water and after about a week out came a lovely green leaf.

In each class room there was a turtle stove, used to heat the rooms. The caretaker used to come in after school to clean it. It was a round iron stove, with a round hole at the top (a special tool was used for this) and the bottom at the front had a little door. The caretaker cleaned the ash out from the bottom, all ready to light the next morning. She also had to fill the scuttle with anthracite, which lasts much longer than coal. The next morning she had to light a fire at the bottom with paper and kindling wood. The room had to be warm in cold weather by the time the children arrived for school.

Before I started school, my three brothers and my sister and me went to Sunday school every Sunday at the Vicarage. A message was sent back to my Mum asking if she would like to take herself and the children to the seaside for the day. She talked it over with Dad and he agreed we should go. We had to meet at Nuffield Church. The coach was full, but I don't really remember very much about it as it was such a long time ago.

I was six years old when war was declared, and I was still in the infant class, still enjoying it and learning all I could, including reading sentences. As a result I was able to take an early reader book home. Willian only had one year left at school by then, so when he wasn't doing anything, Mum asked him to take me to read. The next day I had to take the book back and read it to the teacher.

The nurse used to call every week at school mainly to check the children for head lice. I cannot remember anyone with it. The dentist also called to check our teeth.

Mum had a very difficult labour when my youngest brother, Alf, was born. (Most mothers gave birth at home in those days.) The Midwife called and did as much as she could, but had to call the doctor, who had to come from Woodcote. My brother was eventually born but with a health problem. I didn't know too much about it at the time, but I know he was in Cold Ash Hospital, near Newbury for two years. A Mr Townsend owned the garage at Stoke Row and kindly took my parents to see Alfred every Sunday. Children under 14 weren't allowed in the hospital. Most weeks I went with my parents so Mr Townsend took me to the little sweet shop. I handed my pennies over and I was given a barley sugar stick. I was allowed to eat a little piece. The rest I had to leave until I got home. There Mum took the stick and cut it into four pieces and gave my two brothers and sister each a piece.

My parents were very strict but very fair and everything had to be shared equally. We knew right from wrong at a very early age, never to tell lies, and never ever to buy anything at any time that you couldn't afford. Very good advice and when we all got older, we all understood why.

Alfred was in hospital for two years and then he was much better, and started back to school again. He stayed at Nuffield Primary School until he was 12 years old and was then allowed to leave school.

The war was still on then and I remember knitting scarves and socks for the air force.

We still continued with our other lessons. We all had the same reading book as the teacher, Mrs Witham. She used to start reading and would then pick on any pupil to continue reading. If you didn't get it right, you were kept in at playtime. We went out for a nature walk one day, taking our packed lunch with us. After our nature lesson and after we had had lunch, teacher produced a large hessian sack and we all had to go over the field we were in, collecting *purple clover heads.* We collected a full sack full but I really cannot remember what they were being used for. I can only think it was for something to do with medicine, like poppy heads are used today.

At Christmas time, we used to practise for a concert for the parents to watch. Once I remember being *Little Bo Peep*. I wore a lovely pink dress, and carried a long crook. I used to love acting in plays.

When I was getting on for ten years old I arrived at school to find a wooden frame on both my desk and the girl's desk next to me. We wondered what it was. The teacher told us it was a *loom.* When school started, wool was produced with a comb-like piece of metal. Wool was attached to the frame with the comb placed in the centre, and we could choose which colour wool we wanted. I chose red and yellow.

We were then shown how to start – which was very difficult to begin with. A long needle with an eye – an eye is a long slit so you can thread wool through – was attached to the wool. You lifted the comb up and threaded the wool through. The next row the comb was pressed downwards and the wool threaded through. After a few rows the comb was pulled forward which kept the work even.

Once I got the hang of how to work it, I really enjoyed it. I think I have still got the scarf I made – worn for many, many years and looking very old and weary – like me now.

Another thing we did at that age – we learned to play a game called shinty. This is played with hockey sticks and originated from Scotland. We played with two teams and if the sticks hit your ankles it caused many bruises.

I was ten years old or thereabouts when the war was coming to an end in Europe. The primary school was getting all ready to celebrate with the village. The schoolchildren had to learn songs and dances and plays and use any other talents we had. I remember that it all went off very well and the long wait for peace was coming to an end, but not quite yet.

I had one more year at primary school which made me rather sad as I liked the way we were taught and once taught it stayed learnt. The scholarship exam was coming up in a few months so I used as much time as I could to revise. There was only myself and another girl old enough to sit the exam for the grammar school. When the results came out I passed but the other girl didn't. I was over the moon as I always wanted to go to grammar school and from the age of seven I wanted to be a nurse.

Unfortunately my excitement was short lived and my Mum wasn't happy. She tried to explain that my Dad and she couldn't afford to send me. As today, yes you could get grants, but with so much else to buy going to the grammar school was out of the question. For a few days I was really miserable but with the summer holidays coming up I knew I would be helping a lot on the small holding. I wasn't let off doing my household chores – they had to be done first.

The summer holidays went by very quickly and I was very apprehensive about going to Nettlebed Secondary Modern School, although Charles, John and Ivy had all gone before me. They didn't say much about it.

I enjoyed the first year I was there. I was in Miss Devrows' class and she taught the same way as Nuffield Primary School. Once the first year was finished and I had seemed to be doing very well, things changed. I and another boy seemed to be penalised and not bothered with because our parents could not afford much. Apart from cooking once a week in the next village and doing activities in the Area Sports – the Area Sports were all the different secondary modern schools competing against one another – I was not involved. I came fourth in running and high jump. The rest of the time I couldn't wait to leave school, but before I did leave the Authorities put the school leaving age up from 14 to 15.

In 1947, in one of the worst winters ever that I can remember, with five or six foot snow drifts either side of the road, I was 14 years of age. One time I had just got off the school bus which dropped me at Nuffield when it started to snow – and what a blizzard that was! The roads were getting more and more slippery with the fresh snow, so I had to be very careful not to slip over. My clothes were getting absolutely soaked in no time at all, but I still had a long way to go. It was a two mile walk each way every day. I eventually got to our door and opened it and completely collapsed. Mum, bless her, rushed and picked me up and helped me to a chair in front of a lovely fire and tried to peel my clothes off me. Because it had been so cold coming home my clothes had more or less stuck together, so they were very difficult to get off. Mum also made me some hot milk. I soon revived but what an experience I had had.

I didn't get to school for six weeks after that as the roads were still bad.

People today keep telling me that the 1963-1964 winter was worse. My daughter was born in the latter, and, yes, the roads were bad but you could get around much more easily.

3. Living – and Working with Dad

Good Fridays were a special day for the whole family. All chores were finished early. Mum packed a large basket with all sorts of goodies. Dad then harnessed the horse and we all climbed into the cart and off we went into the underwood where my Dad was working. We were able to play hide and seek around the trees, or my sister and I would go for a walk. If the boys or Mum could help Dad, they would, either by counting out 25 bean rods and putting them in groups for Dad to tie up, or they might carry any over to the cart to be taken home.

Underwood always had to be cut down before the sap rose. My brother John was the one most interested in the things that Dad was doing.

We all sat around a fire in the woods and Dad put on a big kettle in the fire, to fill a big teapot he kept in the woods. Dad always made the tea and had it in the tin mug that he always used. Mum took cups with us and it was really great eating our meal and drinking tea in the woods. When my eldest brother was ill with dementia about six years ago, I reminded him of it. He smiled and said he remembered it too, which really cheered me.

It was a really horrible time, William deteriorating so much, as he and I were the only ones left in the family. William passed away six years ago.

When the field of grass was ready for cutting for hay, Dad had a big scythe (this is a large curved blade) on a long thick rod with two handles. Dad used to go round and round the field cutting the grass. When William and John were old enough they had to get a grass rake, and where Dad had cut, they had to rake the cut grass into rows. When the grass was dry enough it was easier to pick up. The horse was harnessed and attached to the cart. When there was enough hay on the cart, Dad had already made a base to build a hay rick.

With the very hot summers we had in those days, one had to be careful the rick didn't start smoking or catch fire. I remember a few times when the ricks had started to smoke and the whole thing had to be taken back to the ground, and left for a few days before being rebuilt.

When it came to growing a field of potatoes, a two furrow plough had to be attached to the horse.

About a yard from the edge of the field, Dad would straighten the horse and plough and begin to plough. There was an art in this, to keep both the horse and plough in a straight row.

Sacks of seed potatoes were bought and my sister and brothers and me used to put the potatoes about one foot apart – twelve inches or about 30 centimetres – all along the row. When we had finished each row, Dad turned the horse around and covered the potatoes up. Then we would go again and plant another row until the field was planted and the potatoes were all covered up.

During the war years we were allowed two days off school to plant potatoes. I really enjoyed doing this job, and then watched to see the potatoes grow.

Once all the farmers got to know one another they all started to help each other. I know Dad used to leave William and John to get the cows in to milk them while he went off on his bike for the day helping some of the farmers out. When some of the farmers were able to afford machinery, then they would come and help Dad.

I remember the first Fordson tractor and grass cutter that came to the Salt Box with one of the farmers to cut the hay the next year. Oh so much quicker than having to scythe the field.

One day the military arrived and took over half of one of the fields. They dug a long deep trench. This was done for the recruits to use for rifle shooting practice. As well as getting compensation, a few large tins of corned beef came Mum's way.

Once a year Dad was allowed to have a pig killed. The local butcher who lived in Stoke Row did the necessary. He cut all the odd meats – liver, kidneys and so on – ready for use, then he cut two flitches. (A flitch is half a hog or pig.) These were hung salted and cured ready for cutting as needed.

The farmers who had helped Mum and Dad were always rewarded for their work at the small holding with some of the meat. No money changed hands as farmers helped each other equally. Everyone was happy with the arrangement.

When I was about 10 years old, I used to love going with Dad to watch him milk the cows. I enjoy drinking milk but never realised where it came from. One day I asked Dad if he would teach me to milk a cow. Like humans, and all other animals, cows can have different personalities. Dad chose a calm, very patient cow, but warned me that if at any time the cow wasn't happy it would raise its back leg and the bucket would be knocked out of your hand. It took a few times but once I got the hang of it I did it quite often.

My brother John and I were the two people who wanted to learn all the skills that we could connected to the small holding. John was very interested in besom broom making and often used to watch Dad getting all the handles ready. This he could do in the living room which was the only room in the house downstairs that was suitable. Dad showed John the right way to do the shaving of the handles and he also told him to use what Dad called *ash bonds*. These were long straight ash poles shaved very thin like ribbons. So when the silvery birch brush was ready and the handle placed in the middle, Dad had what he called a broom horse. He placed the head and handle across the broom horse. He then tucked the bond through the head, put his feet on the front and gradually tightened the head and handle, turning it and making it tighter as he twisted it around. He could make four or five of these each evening.

My nephew who took to doing this work years later, used wire instead of bonds. Dad said that if one used ordinary wire instead of bonds, it would cut into the broom head over time and wouldn't last nearly as long as bonds.

This was a real craft handed down from his great grandfather and the tools Dad used all came from generations back. John was thrilled to bits when he made his first besom broom properly at the age of 13. Dad was a wonderful patient teacher and John knew then what his future was going to be.

4. Work

My sister had a job at the village grocery shop, but I don't think she was there for very long.

Ivy then applied for a job advertised in the Land Army. She was a cook at Shrivenham in Wiltshire. She was moved about several times and eventually ended up as a cook in Witney, still in the Land Army. I went to stay for a few days and was asked if I would like the job as a domestic help to Ivy. We both stayed until the Land Army was disbanded and no longer required.

The Land Army girls were a lovely crowd. I think there were about 20 in all plus the warden. They worked on different kinds of farms. On seeing some of the girls some farmers weren't very happy saying they couldn't do the work involved but the girls showed them that they could and proved it. Some of the girls who lived close by went home on a day off. One or two of them came home with either Ivy or me – as we were never off at the same time. The girls we took home really enjoyed it. When the land army was coming to the end I remember the warden arranged a farewell party inviting servicemen to join in so there could be dancing. It was a lovely party and Ivy and I had a lovely card of thanks for our hard work.

Ivy soon got another job, but I had to go home for a while.

After the war with so many houses flattened to the ground from the bombing something had to be done and quickly built houses called prefabs were constructed. My friend Pat got very excited about their new home because it had a bathroom which they had never had before. Her mum said it was the best home she'd ever had and they made it so nice and cosy. She lived in Newcastle. Prefabs were going up all over the place as people had to be housed somewhere. The Sheffield steel industry was working flat out to supply the army, navy and air force with all the materials needed for tanks, ships and aeroplanes, plus they had to keep the farmers supplied with the tractors that the Land Girls could use.

Crops were a very essential part of the war effort. Everything was rationed: 2 ounces of butter per week for one person, 4 ounces of sugar. Ta wasn't in bags. It was loose so each household made it go further by using it about three or four times. By the end it was extremely very weak tea! Flour and soap powder were also rationed.

My first job at the post office and shop after the war was when everything was still on ration and everyone including babies had ration books.

Soldiers were just coming back from the war so much had changed while they were away.

Because so much material was used for the war effort there wasn't much available for building more houses. This must have been about 1950. Builders were desperate to build but supplies were so scarce they had to do the best they could with cheaper and not so good materials so therefore the properties being built would not last as long. A lot of the forces coming back from the war were hoping to get their jobs back as a lot of them were still young men

The land army was disbanded. A lot of the land girls went home or a lot of them got married. My sister and I went home for a short time until we both got other jobs which were both living-in jobs.

By that time so much was changing people were making the most of their gardens small or large by growing all kinds of seasonal vegetables. Food was still hard to come by. Families had to be fed and women did a wonderful job making good meals out of what they could. In those days nobody seemed to go hungry. Once the joint was roasted for Sunday and cold for Monday, if there was a bone it used to be boiled with lots of root vegetables added, and also some dumplings. They added pearl barley to thicken it and it made a wonderfully nourishing meal. Children would collect raspberries or blackberries or crab apples from the hedgerows to make a fruit tart or homemade jam or crab apple jelly. Nothing was wasted. Everything was used. Like everything in the steel industry and building industry and other industries like cotton wool and other materials. Very often mum would unpick one jumper or whatever to knit up for something else. Stockings and socks and other clothes were darned if three were any holes. Men's trousers were patched. All this was called *make do and mend*. Yes – you have to give it to mums in those days. Very hard times indeed. A bowl of porridge every morning, bread and jam if you wanted anymore – which the boys often did – a nice cup of tea, and off we went to school, nice and warm inside for the long walk ahead of us.

Somebody called on Mum one as she had heard I was looking for work. I went for an interview the next day and was offered the job as a cook at a fairly big house in one of the next villages. I stayed there for six years before getting married.

Mr and Mrs Balfour of Heath End, Checkendon, were lovely people to work for and very helpful the morning I arrived. They had a lady gardener and two woodmen and a housemaid there. I was very nervous as I was still only 17 years old. My first job each day was to clean out the open fireplace of its ashes and re-lay the fire. I started there in October so there were lovely open fires for a long time ahead. I had to dust and clean it ready to be used later. That room was called the library. I had to get breakfast at 7:00 AM for the gardener and the housemaid and myself. Mrs Balfour had been married before and had a son Peter Stewart. He was in the Fleet Air Arm. Only a very short time after I'd been there I heard he had been awarded the DSO – the Distinguished Service Order. I think it was something to do with shooting down a German plane but I am not 100% sure. They had a lovely big room away from the house where they used to invite all the tenants and their families to a Boxing Day party. That was before I went there. They owned about 9 cottages on the estate. The gardener had a lovely little room across from the back door. Evelyn and I had rooms in the house. Apart from Mr and Mrs Balfour's room, there were three extra bedrooms in the house for guests.

Evelyn was an orphan. She was getting married in the spring. Mr Mrs Balfour bought them a nice little home they could rent in Caversham. Her fiancé, Lou, was a bus driver so it was easy to get to work in Reading. A young girl, Joyce, who had just left school came to replace Evelyn. Joyce did tell me that she really wanted to be a nurse. Joyce knew I had a lot of nursing books and asked if she could borrow them. When she was old enough she applied and was accepted. I'm so pleased to say she did so well and she became a sister. Mr and Mrs Balfour also gave me a lovely 21st birthday party with magic tricks and dancing. I was so pleased my mum and her brother from Kent could come and also my sisters stayed the night.

Mr Balfour had a flat in Earls Court London and the gardener and I used to go with Mr Balfour out of his kindness to shows. He used to pay for us. As it was so many years ago I really can't remember the names of the shows except for one which I could watch over and over again: Bing Crosby and Rosemary Clooney in *White Christmas*. I left two years later with their blessing when I got married.

They came to the wedding and we kept in touch until Mrs Balfour sadly died from cancer. Mabel, the gardener, came to stay wherever we were. Mr Balfour had also passed away but I managed to see him a few weeks before he died to thank him for his kindness to me. Mabel passed away in the War Memorial Hospital in Henley, having moved there after Mr Balfour died. I also kept in touch with Evelyn until she passed away a few years ago.

A few years before we left Ipsden, a lady telephoned me to ask if I could help her elderly mother one morning a week. She said the doctor had recommended me to her. I had to take three references and she introduced me to her mother. I started work for three hours on the Wednesday. She was a lovely lady and told me what she wanted me to do. I didn't have a key to let myself in so I had to knock hard on the door. I suppose I had been there over a year and she told me she was making some sloe gin would I give it a good stir for her. I saw her daughter most weeks as I was about to leave.

One day when I went to work I knocked but got no reply. So I was getting in the car to go to the surgery to see if she was there and I caught a sight of someone in the churchyard opposite. There was Mrs Stobo by one of the graves. She was in her night dress. I took her home and got her dressed, and later made her a nice cup of tea. A few weeks after that time when I couldn't make her hear me knocking, I waited and waited. In the end I went to the churchyard. She wasn't there. I looked around so then decided to go to the surgery to get them to telephone her to see if she was all right. And this they did only for Mrs Stobo to say Mrs Lambert doesn't come on Sundays. The daughter gave me a key after that but unfortunately her mother started getting worse and she went to the Grange nursing home in Goring on Thames.

I went to see her a few times but I was very sorry to hear she had to be moved so they could look after her as much as she needed to be. During that time a message came to ask if I could help an elderly couple out a few doors down from Mrs Stobo. I went to see them as arranged and met their son, Andrew. Oh, they were such a lovely old couple. I started just one afternoon a week as they had cover in the mornings. I used to take Mr Hayes out for a walk to give his wife a break. He had a number of health problems and it must be so hard for an elderly person to look after another one.

The son asked me one day if it would be possible for me to give his dad a strip wash on Saturday mornings. I did this for a number of weeks, and then one day in the week I took Mr Hayes for a walk, When we got home and I had made a cup of tea for us all as usual, Mrs Hayes said she was tired and she was going to have a lie down. I asked if she wanted anything. All she said was, "I'm all right, just tired." I made sure she got into bed all right and she asked if I would make her husband's tea and give it to him. I did as she asked then crept back upstairs to see if Mrs Hayes was all right. She told me she was expecting her daughter to come and she said, "You go home now. You have done enough." I didn't want to leave her so went back down to see if Mr Hayes was having his tea all right. I lingered a while longer as the daughter hadn't shown up. Once again I went back upstairs as I wasn't happy to leave them both. Bless her – she looked so peaceful tucked up in bed. I gave her a kiss on her forehead and told her I was just leaving. I looked in on Mr Hayes once more. He was still enjoying his tea. I wasn't happy leaving with nobody there but I did go. I had a telephone call from Andrew on the Thursday to say his mother had passed away soon after I left. His dad had to go into a nursing home but they did manage to find one quite quickly. I've kept in touch with Andrew and Audrey.

It was after this I started at Cleeve Lodge.

I've also found out the reason we collected purple clover heads when I was at primary school. It was used for medicine to treat asthma, chest pains, breathing problems, skin conditions, osteoporosis and whooping cough. Purple clover is related to the pea and bean family.

Apart from the butcher and the Post Office, there was a baker, Mr Arthur Lambourne, who came to Stoke Row in about 1900, and he moved into a house there in 1905. Mr Lambourne rebuilt a workshop at the property and converted it into a bakery. In 1948 his sons enlarged the bakery. Mr Lambourne was known as the *Midnight Baker* as he often used to deliver bread in the village late into the evening for anyone who needed it. He was also very good at cooking dinners in his bread ovens for the elderly or cooking meals for other people in his ovens if it was too hot to start a range for cooking. There were very hot summers in those days.

His wife had a little shed on the side of the house and whatever children came, either with their parents or on their own, for bread, Annie Lambourne would always see they had a sweet.

Mr and Mrs Lambourne had six boys. Two followed their father into the business, one left home as a baby to live with Mr Lambourne's sister and brother-in-law who couldn't have children, and as they lived in Oxford, it wasn't a million miles away.

All the sons, apart from one, were called up during the War. One was drowned when HMS Gloucester sank, another was a prisoner of war for 4 years 11 months.

When I worked at the Post Office just after I left school, I didn't know a lot of people. On Friday night at about 5.30pm, this man would bring an order for his Mum. As it was Friday night all the other staff had gone home. It was left to me. I read the order all right and placed all the goods on the counter. When he started talking I couldn't understand him as his stammer was so difficult to work out. Eventually between us we managed but I still didn't know who he was. After he had gone I asked the owner of the Post Office who he was and I was told it was Gordon Lambourne from the Bakery and he had only been home from the war a short while after being a prisoner of war (PoW). I knew of the Lambourne family but didn't know them personally.

My first job at 15 years old was for 17 shillings and 8 pence – about 88p in decimal currency. Out of this I gave Mum 10 shillings for my keep – 50p. it took ages to save £5 for a new coat. This taught me the value of money – something that I wish some parents would teach their children today.

When I was cook at Heath End, Checkendon, Cecil Lambourne started delivering bread to them. I asked him how Gordon was, but he had already left home and was working in the government of the ESSO Petroleum Company at Harwell. He was there quite a while and enjoyed his work. And learned to play lawn bowls. One day I received a letter from Gordon telling me all about where he was working, so much about nature, and he wondered if I would keep in touch. I did and I realised that his stammer was caused by his dreadful war when so many lives were lost, with wounded troops coming home so weak and weary, wondering what their lives would be like. It was so difficult for some of them to settle and when I hear of old ex-soldiers sleeping on the streets, I feel so sad. Nobody will ever know what these people went through, partly because so many don't want to talk about it. But well done to the 90+ age group to go to schools and try to get through to the children just how bad it was.

Gordon's Mum died on 23rd April 1956. We were now going out together and became engaged in June that year. I was still working at Checkendon so I didn't get much time off. When Gordon came down to see me one Saturday afternoon, I introduced him to Mr and Mrs Balfour. They were very pleased to meet him and asked him if he would like to stay for supper, which he did from then on every Saturday night, when he was home for the weekend.

5. Gordon and Me

Houses were being built at this time. Gordon enquired if he would be able to get a mortgage but was told that his wages wouldn't allow it. Every time we heard about a house any where we tried for it. Our only option there was a tied house, which is a house that goes with a job. The only one we found was at Shiplake, near Henley on Thames. Gordon was offered the job. I think we were there about 18 months.

We cycled from Shiplake to the Salt Box every weekend to see Mum and Dad and then on the way home called to see Gordon's Dad.

Edna's Mother, Gordon's Father, Gordon, Edna and Edna's Father

We arranged to get married on 19th December as Gordon was getting so unhappy with his lodgings. It wasn't a big wedding, just family and friends and a small reception in Stoke Row Village Hall. St John's Church in Stoke Row was quite full, I remember, as so many people knew both families. My outfit was a pale blue two piece with little silver threads going through it.

Edna and Gordon

I was much younger than Gordon but to us it didn't matter. We loved each other and we knew it would work out all right.

We attended church at Shiplake most Sundays and as Gordon knew a little old lady a few doors away, I used to cook her a meal.

As time went on I was offered a few hours work each week in a lovely big house on the river called

Sagamore. I believe Vince Hill, the singer, used to live there. Unfortunately I used to get laryngitis a lot and the doctor told me that we were living too close to the river.

Gordon then applied for a job at Checkendon Court as a gardener and he was given the job. We both loved it there and I also worked in this big house which was owned by Mr and Mrs Rothbath. Before her marriage Mrs Rothbath was Helena Pickard, the actress who appeared in many films with Bing Crosby and Bob Hope. Her son is Edward Woodward who used to act in a lot of war films, including *The Great Escape*.

I saw so many famous faces though I cannot remember them all now.

They had a spinet – a type of piano – in the hall and one celeb who came down often played it so well.

Gordon loved his job and it had made a big difference that he had known the head gardener so well as he was a Stoke Row man too.

Gordon's speech was getting much better by this time but he was still very unsure about anyone he didn't know.

Mrs Rothbath died a few years after we started working there and a few years after that Mr Rothbath was killed early one morning in a car accident going down St Peter's Hill in Caversham. Mr Rothbath had a daughter by his first marriage so we thought she might take over Checkendon Court, but she had moved into a much smaller house in Lovegrove Lane in Checkendon, and was starting up a riding stables.

Checkendon Court was then sold and the people who bought it brought their own staff so we had to move out. We were offered Meadow Cottage in the village but only until we could find other employment. By this time I had a son, Stephen, who was only 6 weeks old. We tried desperately to find something but nobody wanted us with a baby as they wanted me to work in the house. Eventually we found a two bedroom bungalow in Hambleden, near Henley and Gordon would be working for an elderly lady.

In 1962 my Dad sadly passed away in Townlands Hospital, Henley, with bronchial pneumonia. I was absolutely devastated as I loved my Dad so much. I also had just found out that I was pregnant again.

My daughter was born on 9th January 1963, a tiny 5lbs 4 oz in weight. We called her Rosemary.

When Rosemary was just about over a year old, a knock came on the front door. A gentleman stood there – Gordon was at work – and I sort of knew his face but couldn't put a name to it. When he came in, he said that the reason he was here was that he wondered if Gordon would like a gardening job at Ipsden House, where he lived. We had thought that we might have to move anyway as the bungalow was so damp. Gordon went for an interview one Sunday morning, and after looking over the house that went with the job, Gordon accepted the offer of the job.

When he told the boss that he was working for, she tried so hard to keep him, even saying that she would have a new house built for us.

My Mum had passed away on 2nd January exactly two years after my Dad. She had a massive stroke and died in bed. My brother, Alf, was living with them at the time but unfortunately had gone to the doctor's to get her some tablets.

What a shock for us as a family.

We were such a great family with so many happy memories. Alf took Mum's death very badly and we all had to watch him very carefully. After some time he got himself a job with the Forestry Commission and he was there for 30 years and was very popular.

After we were married I booked tickets to see a show in London. It was a matinée, and was called *The Bride and the Batchelor*, with a well-known actress, Cicely Courtneidge alongside Jack Hulbert. It was such a funny show and it was really good to hear Gordon laugh so much. I just wish that I could have taken him to see more shows but money just wouldn't allow it. Gordon was only getting £5 per week plus the house to live in, and that wasn't very much even in those days. We had to buy all our vegetables as there was no garden to grow anything. We used to sit together in the evenings listening to lovely soft, relaxing music, which we both liked.

When we moved to Hambledon, we used to take the bus with Stephen when it was Henley Regatta Saturday, and sit watching the boats enjoying our picnic on the river bank. When Rosemary was born we did the same thing and Gordon and I found it so relaxing. We didn't have a television until 1964, and then it was, of course, only black and white and rented as we couldn't afford to buy one.

Gordon loved Christmas and what it really meant and when we moved to Ipsden our next door neighbour, Mrs Campbell, used to look after the children while we went to the midnight service at Checkendon church. The church was always full of people from the villages around. Everyone greeted everyone else and the service was always very moving and peaceful. On the way home frost was white on the ground and sparkling, and as we got nearer home we could see Didcot Power Station lit up with its blue and green lights, plus all the lights of the houses in the distance. How blessed we were to see such views.

When we moved to Ipsden and Gordon had a Saturday off, we often booked a day trip to Weymouth. Before the children were born I remember we had a week's holiday on the Isle of Wight. Before we had a car, Gordon used to bike to Wallingford to get his hair cut. One day he came home and told me that he had booked a Sunday trip to Hereford and Evesham, lunch included, for the four of us. It was such a lovely day. The views were absolutely stunning. We went into Hereford Cathedral – what a beautiful place that is with all the lovely carvings and the care that went into it all. Gordon loved looking in churches or cathedrals.

Before we were married and when he worked for the Esso Petroleum Company, his name came out of a draw with about 29 other people to go to the coronation of Elizabeth 11. What a wonderful day that must have been for him. What with the crowds of people, the carriages and how beautiful she looked with all the military on parade. This was another thing that Gordon and I enjoyed. Nobody does this like Great Britain.

I saw it on television at Heath End, Checkendon and this was my first time of seeing something on television. I remember it so vividly to this day – and remember that the shops were hiring out televisions for that one occasion – again only in black and white.

We rented our first television in 1964. The children loved watching the children's programmes like *Andy Pandy*, *The Wombles* and *Blue Peter*. When *Blue Peter* had a lot of their old coins stolen once, we sent some of our old ones to them. They sent a thank you letter back to Stephen and Rosemary with two postcards of Valerie Singleton, Christopher Trace and their beautiful dog, Shap. The children were so pleased and I think it taught them to try to help wherever you can.

We used to watch *Morecambe and Wise*, *Steptoe and Son*, *Dad's Army*, *Terry and June* and *The Good Life* – all the programmes that made us laugh – plus the more serious programmes like *Songs of Praise* and nature programmes. Gordon loved *Countryfile* and *One Man and his Dog*. If there was a good film on, we used to watch it.

By this time the children were growing up. Stephen was into all kinds of sport. He joined a cricket club in Goring, until he and a mate got a team together in Ipsden. He was into football, darts and something called Aunt Sally. We were pleased he was having a social life as Rosemary was the outgoing one.

If anyone reads this I'm sure they must think what a dull life we led, but Gordon and I liked the simple life, where there was no hustle and bustle and no crowds to deal with.

If we went shopping, especially at Christmas time, you didn't have people barging into you.

For many years we had up to ten people for Christmas Lunch. I made my own Christmas puddings and cake, and with Stephen's help I still do, following a 70 year old recipe.

In the afternoons we played a game called *Shove Halfpenny* or Dominoes or Draughts, and we always watched the Queen's speech. On Christmas mornings at about 12 noon, Mr and Mrs Campbell would come round to us for a drink or we would go round to them. We took it in turns. Their children were older than ours but we all got on as neighbours as most people did then.

Gordon had bought a greenhouse and he loved growing his own vegetables from seed. Any surplus vegetables were given away to neighbours. Christopher, Rosemary's son, used to love going to see Grandad in the greenhouse or watching him plant seedlings out.

Soon after we moved to Ipsden we used to go to a place called Mattocks in Sutton Courtney. They used to grow acres and acres of roses – all different types and colours. Gordon wanted to make a rose garden in the front garden. We already had a lovely herbaceous border. Gordon used to pick all the roses out he wanted while he could see the flowers, then when it was the right time to plant them in the late autumn, Mattocks used to write to him and tell him they were ready to collect. They were all bare root plants.

Gordon made the most lovely rose garden and the scent was wonderful.

In 1974 Gordon's health was beginning to show signs of deteriorating in his walking and for the next few years he was struggling. He was in pain with his legs, but wouldn't give in. I used to take him to the doctor three times a week to get his foot re-dressed and the nurse came out at weekends. He used to potter about outside in the garden. My daughter was living with us at the time with her baby son, Christopher. Christopher was so pleased when he went to help Grandad and Grandad Gordon adored Christopher.

We didn't really know what was wrong with Gordon's legs. He was sent to a London hospital to try and help him but they couldn't do anything for him. I took him to the doctor one Friday morning. Bless him he could hardly walk but he insisted on walking to the car. The doctor took one look at his leg and said he had to go to hospital.

This was only in the morning, so he told us to go home, have a cup of tea and he would get the ambulance with us at 11.30 a.m.. Gordon sat by the front door smoking his pipe knowing, as I did, he wouldn't be home again. We knew each other so well – same music, same sense of humour, knowing what each other was going to say, sharing the last chocolate or cake.

It was the thing marriage was all about. We knew that 27 wonderful years were coming to an end. The memories were there and couldn't be taken away. If only children today had memories like that.

We all used to go to Margate in Kent for our holidays each year. The children loved it so much and it is lovely remembering Gordon building sand castles with them.

Christopher wanted to see Grandad as much as he could and would sit on his hospital bed drawing pictures for him.

When Gordon went into hospital John used to phone me every night to see how he was. Gordon and John got on so well together. He was Gordon's best man at our wedding and we were godparents to his kids..

Gordon's gangrene was getting worse. The surgeons tried everything possible to stop it spreading up his leg and in the end they had to amputate his leg above the knee. Unfortunately it kept spreading. In his last two weeks he didn't know we were there but I kept talking to him, hoping he would know I was there.

He sadly passed away on 7th September 1984, seven weeks to the day after entering hospital. Like his parents before him he was buried in Stoke Row Church Yard, where we could tend his grave.

It has been 38 years now since Gordon passed away and I still miss him so much.

As I sit quietly after doing a few small jobs with a nice hot drink, I think back to when I got married and moved into our first home. It was the first house in a row of cottages. All the neighbours were so nice and friendly. We had chats at the garden gate. Each time we moved it was the same. Families were families, neighbours were neighbours. Neighbours inviting each other for a cup of tea and a chat.

After the funeral I started back to work. Stephen had started his new job at the Post Office the June before, and we both thought that work would help.

A few weeks after the funeral I was asked if I would be interested in the caretaker's job at the local school, and as it was just down the road, I accepted and stayed for 6 years. At the same time I was offered a cleaning job in the village.

In spite of this I still felt empty inside and felt I needed a challenge. The Royal Berkshire Hospital in Reading – where Gordon had passed away – wanted to build a radiotherapy unit. I contacted the hospital. They visited me, and with the date of their choice I organised a sale in the garden.

I had never done anything like it before.

When I told my sister and my three brothers they were really willing to come and help. One or two friends also joined in as well. I was really hoping that I wouldn't have clothes to sell, but so many clothes came, I couldn't refuse.

So with bric-à-brac, a massive cake stall, raffle, teas and coffees and John with his besom brooms, we made £600. They were so pleased they asked us if I would do it next year, and that year we raised over £1,000. After that I did small coffee mornings for the Church or the Cricket Club, then Sue Ryder and Sobell House in Oxford.

We made use of one of the vegetable plots in the garden by planting as much veg as we could. We lived in a semi-detached house, built in memory of Mr Remnant's son, Ben, who was killed in the Second World War.

Our next door neighbours were Mr and Mrs Campbell who lived in the side of the house built for an invalid. Our side was for the gardener of Ipsden House.

I still had lots of work which mainly consisted of helping elderly people who couldn't cope on their own and a young lady of 35 who had cancer.

After the elderly people and Louise, the lady with cancer, passed away, I applied for a job in a Care Home in Goring on Thames. I absolutely loved it there with most in their 90s and one who was 106 years old. I was there for 6 years and I was rather sad when the owner said she was retiring to Salisbury with her husband. Someone else took over and, sadly, it wasn't the same. I stayed for three months.

Then I had a few hours a week working for an elderly lady in Stoke Row. When she was not able to stay there even with two carers and myself, her son made arrangements for her to go to a Nursing Home in Cambridgeshire. Unfortunately she was very unhappy there as it was too far away for any of her friends to go and see her.

In between I did the Ipsden Cricket Club teas for 6 years.

6. Moving to Didcot

Ten years ago Stephen was able to afford a mortgage to get his own property, and after 49 years in Ipsden we had a lot of downsizing to do. The roses were too big and old to move, so we couldn't take any with us. Stephen managed to find a nice little house on the outskirts of Didcot. We were very pleased to leave to leave Ipsden. Yes – the views were stunning but adding everything up it was the right thing to do. We have never missed Ipsden, and all the time my brother was alive that was the only reason we went back.

All our friends and family love the house and often tell Stephen he did the right thing.

Gordon unfortunately didn't see the house we moved to but before he got too weak to walk far, Stephen used to take him for a ride round in the summer evenings. Gordon loved and appreciated that.

One rose that Gordon chose for the rose garden was *Ena Harness* – a very old rose variety with a wonderful scent. After we left Ipsden I tried to get one and tried garden centres everywhere as my friends loved that variety too. I spoke to Andy at Root One and he told me that it was such an old rose, I wouldn't be able to get one. I used to receive plant and seed catalogues from Jersey and to my delight looking through one, there was the *Ena Harkness* rose. I have now had it in the back garden by our back door for nearly four years now. The scent is still wonderful and it still blooms until November.

We always watched the *Service of Remembrance* in the evening before the service at the Cenotaph on the Sunday nearest to the 11th November.

On Christmas Eve both Gordon and I worked when he was the gardener at Ipsden House and I was the caretaker, but he was home much earlier than I was. Mr and Mrs Crosthwaite, who lived at Ipsden House always had people in for drinks. I was never late back but when I arrived home Gordon had peeled the potatoes and prepared the Brussel sprouts all ready for the next day. And he had also cleaned the red tiles that made up the kitchen floor.

He was so thoughtful.

Stephen follows after him in so many ways but I don't have people for Christmas Lunch any more.

Those days are long gone but the memories of so many friends and family are still there. When we were still at Ipsden my brother John didn't have a television so he used to bring his family over for Christmas afternoon. There was always a circus on and the children loved it.

When we moved to Didcot 10 years ago Stephen and I walked into town for a few bits we needed. A man in the house next to ours was washing his car. He introduced himself as Alan so we introduced ourselves. He said what a lovely quiet friendly place it was. He said they had only moved in six months before. His wife was busy but came out to say hello. Her name was Jean. They had a little dog called Ronnie and, oh, he made such a fuss of us. What a lovely welcome from all three.

Alan and Jean had apparently lived somewhere in Didcot before and they also had a family in Didcot. They had moved from Dorset so that they could be nearer to their family, which was a son and daughter, grandchildren, and great grandchildren. One really happy family.

When I was 62, Stephen surprised me by saying he had booked a holiday in Jersey. We would be going by plane from Southampton airfield. Everything was arranged by Tappins, the travel agents in Wallingford. After so many years not having a holiday at all, I now wanted to travel more. We have been twice to Jersey, twice to Ireland and three times to Scotland, plus many other parts of the south of England.

Stephen and I were still living at Ben's Cottages in Ipsden. I was now able to rent it from Mr Reader who owned most of the Ipsden Estate. The rent was very small and he was very good in getting repairs done, particularly as it was a memorial cottage.

When he died he had no family to leave Ipsden Estate to, so it was passed on to a lady relative. After about six months following her take over of the estate, the rents started increasing – mine by £16 for 4 weeks. This went on for a few years and no repairs were done, and the rent went up every two years. The house was subsiding and this cracked the one inch thick window sills which broke in half. It became so damp and cold I just couldn't keep it warm. All we had, apart from the electric fires we bought, were two open fires. One day I had Saville's, the house agents, round to look round it. She looked at it and asked me how on earth I could live in it. I said – with difficulty.

Stephen was keen to get his own house. He was still working for the Post Office. He had tried to save as much as he could from when he left school. And I have to say that the insurance agent we had at that time was extremely good and advised him where to put his money to get the best interest. In about 2009 he had two reasonable policies that had matured, so he went to the Nationwide Building Society in Henley to talk to them about a mortgage. Of course they could only offer him a certain amount.

Stephen tried so hard to find somewhere around the area but it was far too expensive. I couldn't help as all the money I earned went on rent and council tax, plus coal to keep warm. The only other place to look was Didcot. He tried several estate agents one Monday morning to be told the same thing: two bedroom houses were hard to find. As he was leaving one estate agent, the agent put a paper on the desk and said that they had got this one – a three bedroom house – and Stephen should take it home and see what we thought.

When he got home and threw the paper on the table, I said it wouldn't hurt to go and see it. We got an appointment for the same Monday afternoon and met the estate agent there. When she opened the door it was so lovely and warm and cosy looking – and all the furniture was there. It had been beautifully decorated and I fell in love with it, straightaway. Stephen still wasn't sure, so he rang his very good friend, Simon, to ask if he would look at it too, and advise him.

Simon and his wife, Donna, met with the estate agent on the Wednesday morning. Simon could only see a couple of things that needed doing – a two ridge tiles and one other minor thing. Simon suggested that Stephen should go for it. They talked over a price and told the estate agent. After a few days talking to the relatives of the person who owned it, Stephen's offer was accepted.

We had to keep quiet about it until contracts were exchanged.

After that we had to think of down-sizing. A lot of the furniture I had was ruined by the damp and cold house in Ipsden. We had lived at Ben's Cottage for 49 years so there was so much to get rid of and as the last of Gordon's brothers had passed away and that house hadn't been cleared. Gordon's parents, the Lambournes, had started living there in the 1900s, so 100 years of stuff had to be cleared.

Gordon's brother didn't leave a proper will and as he wasn't married, Stephen, Rosemary and a nephew in London were the only relatives left. The hospital telephoned to tell us to get in for midday. I rang Basil to be told he would come down to Ipsden and we could all go in his car. As time got nearer to 12, no Basil turned up. I rang him again – they had to have breakfast. Stephen and I said we cannot wait and we got in the car and started off. We arrived rather late to be told that all Cecil's organs were closing down and nothing could be done for him. We had to make a decision for the hospital to turn his ventilator off. According to Basil's wife it had to be my decision, and with hesitation I said yes. When we left the hospital, Basil wanted us all to go to the Bakery as he wanted to find Cecil's will.

Cecil had told me that he had made his will through the British Legion but in actual fact he hadn't made a proper will. Basil kept looking until he found a small piece of paper with what he wanted done with the Bakery. He wanted it sold. It badly needed modernising. Several people went to view it but only a few were interested.

Cecil was buried in Stoke Row churchyard. My daughter and I cleaned the Bakery from top to bottom on the Saturday morning before the funeral on the Wednesday.

Basil's idea was to buy a few sandwiches at M&S as he didn't expect many people to come. I told him that he had no idea as I knew there would be at least 100 people there. He was so shocked. Basil made a great performance at the undertaker's office, not wanting any of the dates for the funeral that they offered – Stephen and I would have gone along with the first one they offered – and in the end it was the third date or the vicar couldn't do it.

£380 was found under the bedroom carpet and the estate agent sent it on to Basil.

Stephen, Rosemary and I did all the catering for the funeral tea. All the people who came thought it was lovely to hold it actually at the bakery, where they could wander round enjoying looking at all the old family photographs handing on the walls and so many other valuable things. Basil and his wife and son never helped serve any of the teas, so we were unable to mingle with people like they did.

As people left they thanked the three of us for such a wonderful tea. Stephen and I went over two days later to start clearing and to our horror Basil had taken every picture and everything of any value back to London. He had seen hardly anything of his uncle. He had come down once near the end and taken him shopping. Cecil had left Stephen, Rosemary and me a small legacy but the majority went to Basil. He never told us how much he made on what he took back to London. I think it is so sad people just want one thing out of people's death and are never grateful.

7. Gordon's War

I often wondered when Gordon told me that although the War might have ended in 1945 for some but not for us, he didn't get home until 1946. It was no good me asking what he meant, as he wouldn't have told me.

Last year I was told that I could apply to get my husband's War Records. I don't do emails or online contacts, just pen and paper, and just as I was about to start my next door neighbour, Jenny, came in. she took out her phone and told me she would do it for me. She asked me what Gordon's army number was. I couldn't tell her – all I could tell her was the camp he was in. I had to send a copy of our marriage certificate and also Gordon's death certificate to prove I was next of kin. In about March or April in 2022 I did receive his War Records. On reading them I can understand the stammer and the horrible nightmares and flashbacks he went through. In today's world things would be so different, and all those who suffered would get help, but not in 1945-46. I do know it was very difficult for a lot of men to settle down into civilian life again.

Gordon's War Records showed that he worked in several coal mines, a paper mill and he helped to build a railway line. All these things must have been very hard work, and I also know that they were given odd boots or two left boots.

All that work as well as long marches and next to no food at the end of the day. Mainly cabbage soup and half a slice of bread. If they could they would find vegetable peelings in bins to eat.

Even reading the report and hearing from other prisoners I just cannot imagine what it would be like to go through it. I firmly believe it was Gordon's faith that got him through as he was only five foot two inches tall (157 cms) and only weighed 8 stone (50.8 kilograms).

His last camp was one that the Germans built for British PoWs right next to Auschwitz. On reading this I knew that Gordon's time there must have been very hard, as it must have been to see so many of his mates collapse and die in front of his eyes and not be able to help. They just had to leave them where they died.

One day last year I bought a book all about Auschwitz. I have no idea what made me buy this book. When I started reading it I found it the most horrific experience one could get. How people could treat other human beings so wickedly is beyond me. Pure evil.

As I read more into the book, I couldn't believe my eyes. At the top of the page was Stalag VIIIB. This was the camp where my husband had been a prisoner of war. Gordon didn't talk about the war and all he told me was that on one wet day when marching from one camp to another, he had dropped his case with all his belongings. He wasn't allowed to pick it up. He would have been shot or bayonetted in the back. He also said that he had worked on a railway. That was all he ever told me.

I received his war records in about March or April this year – 2022. It only mentioned that he was in 7 different camps: he worked in a paper factory; down a coal mine; and on that railway.

He had been captured in France in 1940 and was only released in 1946, well after the end of the war. He had had to march all the way back to France where a plane was waiting to take him to England. They had to march in all weathers – rain, snow, freezing cold, and icy – in odd boots of all different sizes on their feet, or even two left boots.

It was no wonder that his legs and feet were so bad and painful as he got older.

I can't imagine how painful it must have been before they had a short break from marching miles and miles.

Their legs must have been very painful with every step they took.

When we met up with Gordon's PoW mate, Bill, about 12 years after the war, Bill wanted to talk about what had happened to them until Gordon stopped him. Bill did mention that Gordon was marched out of the camp one night and the rest of the men thought that he was going to be shot. They were relieved when Gordon came back into camp.

8. Living

John and I used to visit each other as often as we could. One day he told me that he had to go to the doctor at Sonning Common. It was very unusual for John to mention doctors let alone go and see one. He was having trouble with his breathing and the doctor sent him to the Royal Berks Hospital. I was absolutely shattered when he told the family that he had lung cancer. He was sent to London to have a check and they explained everything to him.

My brother Bill and I went up to London to see him. Like we all do, he wanted to get home, but living on his own wasn't possible so his daughter Bridget stayed with him until he felt he could manage. I went over as often as I could to do some cleaning for him. I thought he was doing so well until he had to go for a check up. Unfortunately the cancer was spreading to the other lung and the hospital couldn't do anything more for him. He was admitted to the Sue Ryder Home at Nettlebed where he sadly passed away on 8th April at around 3.00am.

I was woken up to be told the news from the Sue Ryder Home. I was so pleased to think that we, my brothers, my sister and I, were all round his bedside the day before. We had all gone back to have a nice cup of tea at my younger brother, Alf's. it was so nice to be all together.. As John's cottage was rented, everything had to be cleared out. Animals were given new homes. Bill and Alf, with John's son Mark cleared the sheds. Bridget, Mark's wife Penny and I cleared the house.

John was buried in Stoke Row churchyard not too far away from Gordon's gave. We all missed John so much as a family, but we all kept in touch with one another. As my sister lived further away we took it in turns to telephone each other.

It took a long time for it to sink into my mind when I was told that my lovely sister Ivy had died of a massive heart attack less than a year after John. That same afternoon I was asked to go to Bill's as Ivy's husband would be there. I just couldn't stop crying and so couldn't say much. It appeared that the Trent family wanted Ivy to be buried at Stoke Row with the rest of the family. My sister had lived right opposite the church at Tetsworth. When I went to stay with he we always went to church there. Because of the different counties it all had to be given the go ahead by the Bishop of Oxford. The funeral service was in Tetsworth church and we then went on to Stoke Row churchyard to bury Ivy, right next to John.

Ivy passed away on 22nd March 1994.

Bill and Alf saw a lot of each other after Ivy's death. Alf used to bring us lots of wood to Ipsden to keep us warm. I used to go and see him as often as I could. When I went to see him one day, he asked if I had seen Bill. My answer was, "No, not today." The I asked why and if there was something wrong. He had wanted Bill to tell me that he also had cancer. It was different from John's as the hospital couldn't do anything at all for him.

My daughter, Rosemary, went over to do his cleaning or anything else she could do for him. MacMillan Nurses were very good and often visited him or telephoned to see how he was. He went to the Sue Ryder Home for a while to sort out his tablets or see if they could do anything for him. Alf had an open fireplace at his bungalow, and he loved his open fires. I felt this was a golden opportunity to get his chimney swept, but I really didn't want to interfere as he was seeing a lot more of Bill and his family. I went to see him most days at the Sue Ryder Home and often went to the bank in Henley for him.

When he came home after a few days, he lit his fire and the chimney caught fire. Alf was getting quite poorly by then and couldn't move about quickly. By the time he rang Bill the smoke had got into his throat, which didn't help at all. A few weeks after I went to see him one Sunday afternoon. When I got there people were standing around. I knew most as family and friends. When I went inside my daughter and her children were there. I really thought something had happened. I thought all these people were far too many at one time. I stayed a short while to talk to Alf. I could see that he didn't want so many people there, so I just kissed him and said I will come in tomorrow.

As I left I spoke to Ken, whom we both knew well. I hadn't been home many minutes when the phone rang. It was Ken to tell me that Alf had taken a turn for the worse and he was coughing up blood. Would I go back?

I must admit that when I got there, the doctor didn't look pleased to see so many people there. The doctor rang the Sue Ryder Home for him to be admitted straightaway. I told him that I would come and see him the following day, which I did. I stayed with him for a few hours. The next morning I rang the Home. Apparently they had called Bill in on the Monday night, but I didn't know. I picked my daughter up and went over. Bill and his youngest daughter were there. He had gone down so fast since I had seen him the day before. We stayed as long as we could but had to get back for my granddaughter who was at primary school.

Alf sadly passed away about 6.00pm that day, 6th February 1995, aged just 65. Three family members had died in less than three years. That was really hard to take. Just the eldest and youngest left from one lovely big family.

Grieving can take people in so many different ways. With both his brothers gone, Bill went completely silent on me. He wouldn't speak to me for a few years. I saw him several times. It had to take him longer to talk to me but knowing Bill, I wouldn't rush him. I knew he would eventually start talking.

That was one of the hardest things I have had to face.

One afternoon, Stephen and I were having a cup of tea. I looked out of the window and saw Bill arriving in his three wheeler car. I opened the front door and said, "How nice to see you. Come in. you must have smelt the tea pot." That's a favourite saying of ours. He brought me a lovely bunch of flowers and some tomatoes he had grown.

Thank goodness I had got my brother back.

9. Some Context

In 1953 Roger Bannister broke the record for the first man to break the four minute mile at the Horsepath running track in Oxford.

Lots of sport was coming back after the war and this was good to see after such a gloomy five years of war. The industries were all doing well and in the late 1950s and early 1960s good materials were now being made.

In 1966 England won the football World Cup which was hosted by England at Wembley Stadium. The manager was Alf Ramsey. The players worked each day in their various jobs and England won the final match 4 goals to 2 playing Germany. This has never been achieved since in spite of so many different managers trying. I remember watching it on television with my husband. It was a very exciting game.

One of the biggest changes in my lifetime came on February 15th 1971 when Great Britain changed from pounds, shillings and pence to decimal currency. In primary school we were taught 12 pence made one shilling, twenty shillings made one pound and so on. To me and so many elderly people we found it so confusing to change. For instance we were used to paper one pound notes and paper ten shilling notes. Ten shillings was half of a pound.

We had to get used to one pound coins. Paper money was phased out later on apart from £20, £10 and £5 notes. The liquid measurements also had to change to litres. There was no more *two pints make one quart, four quarts make one gallon* and so on. Distance measurements had to change too and we no longer had inches, feet or yards anymore. We had to use metres. To this day I still haven't worked that one out. You couldn't go into a shop and say you would like one yard of material. It had to be metres or centimetres.

Butchers and market traders all had to change. Thanks to my butcher and market trader as they haven't changed. I can ask for a pound of mince and they still know what I want. Of course they have both been doing it for so long – in fact I've known both for at least 50 years and as for Peter the vegetable trader, I knew his dad when he owned the market stall.

Another change on came on August the 28th 1994 when Sunday trading was legalised and shops could open on Sunday from 10:30 AM to 4:30 PM.

A very sad day came in 1997 when Diana, Princess of Wales, died after a car crash in Paris. She was 36 years old and she left Prince William at 15 and Prince Harry at 12 without their mother.

For many years the NHS was really struggling to cope with so many patients needing all kinds of different treatments. The NHS was being stretched to the limit. I have been hearing how bad it was getting so many times but I just couldn't believe it was so bad. Much of the trouble was called bed blocking which really meant patients were not well enough to be home on their own but too well to be in hospital.

Then in 2019 people started going down with flu-like symptoms but it was much worse than flu and it was called COVID-19. So many people died from it. The awful thing was that relatives were unable to be with their loved ones at the hospital at the end of their lives for fear of spreading COVID further. Hospitals were now overcrowded and so many were treated in corridors. People were asked not to have party gatherings at home for fear of spreading it even further but some people totally ignored this and went on as usual. Finally a breakthrough came when a vaccine was found to work. Some people suffered more than others from the vaccine but on the whole people felt well again after a few days.

Many supermarkets had been built by now and people were finding they could buy much more for their money. Fridge freezers were being bought so one could put meat and fish in them to keep it for later which saved going out to the local shops so often. In many ways I was very sad and I'm sure other people felt the same as I did for the simple reason the small local village shop could not keep up with so much competition. So many shops were closing because of it and therefore all the personal service we were used to was all disappearing. This again was sad for many elderly people who used to have a conversation with the shopkeeper as in a good number of villages the shopkeeper was the hub of the village. They knew everyone and their families and always asked how everyone in the family was.

On about the 5th of September 2022 the Queen was in residence in Balmoral in Scotland. She had seen Boris Johnson when he resigned as Prime

Minister. The next day the queen inducted Liz Truss to be Prime Minister. On September the 8th 2022 Queen Elizabeth sadly passed away. I had been about four or five years old when I heard about King George V passing away. Then came the abdication of the Duke of Windsor which meant his brother had to take over as King George VI. Queen Elizabeth reigned for 70 years. I used to buy every book I could find when Elizabeth and her sister Margaret were children. Such an interesting family and some wonderful pictures too.

I was just out of isolation from Covid and was able to watch the Queen's journey to Westminster Abbey where she would be guarded by the royal family overnight before her final journey to Windsor Castle, and then being laid to rest with the rest of the royal family. For me it was very emotional because the queen had reigned for so long and done such wonderful work.

Nearly every time I get taken for a coffee or meal and elderly people are together, their conversations go back to our old days and the differences between then and now. We are now in the 21st century but to us we're going backwards no loyalty, no respect – honestly it seems to be all jealousy, selfishness and greed now. To me the culprits are the people at the top in their big offices, their flash cars and their big houses – often more than one. Whatever profit there is from industry now seems to be going into their pockets.

Where are all the bonuses going that the workers in shops and offices used to get? They don't get anything like that anymore. I was often told years ago how much people appreciated their bonuses. They were usually about January and they used to pay the winter bills with it. It all helped them so much. Now it's like Big Brother watching or tracking the young to see where they are. Years ago jobs used to be done properly: roads were maintained so potholes were hardly ever seen. Thames Water used to be very efficient. If you called them out they came, but not anymore. When my son bought the property 10 years ago he asked for a water meter to be fitted. 10 years later we still haven't got it. Three different people have had meters put in near us but because they know our old meter is under the tarmac near the road they are too idle to do it. It has already been marked out by one of their colleagues where it should be.

It is very sad to think everything is in such a mess. Greenbelt land is now being used for housing. Builders are building on floodplains. This is the reason for all the flooding in houses. Apart from all the illness this is causing through damp and mouldy walls.

The NHS is a shambles in spite of what it was meant to be when it was started.

Far too many people know how to work the system. It comes back again and again – that word greed.

As a family we used to love walking by the river on Sunday afternoons in the summer, but now with all the rubbish which gets left about and so much unwanted materials just thrown away it all looks horrible. And unkempt. Whenever I mentioned this I'm told they don't have enough staff so why then are all the bosses cutting down on staff? A simple answer more money in their pockets.

When the Royal Mail was privatised – that was the worst thing possible thing. From the start stamps started shooting up in price and now stamps are so expensive elderly people aren't receiving birthday or Christmas cards anymore because people can't afford to buy stamps. I know how much it means to elderly people to receive a card from people or relatives who have moved away. The fat cats don't care about older folk – they would like to get rid of us all. Parcels and packages make them far more profits.

As we all part and go our different ways we say our days, were hard, money wasn't so good but it went further. We certainly had the best years.

One thing I'm really looking forward to at the end of April beginning of May is the bluebells. They should be appearing with the beautiful green of the leaves in the beechwoods, carpets of bluebells and maybe a few wood anemones in between, I used to pass these woods every day when I was working and I would often stop the car to admire them. Such beauty. My son has promised to take me and I will be able to see the bluebell woods once again not too far from where I grew up. Something I will look forward to.

When I look back on my life my goodness how times have changed. So many changes that are good and some not so good. I just couldn't believe hearing some schools buying cereals and fruit to give children breakfast before they start lessons. It has also changed in schools. My primary school teacher used to walk round the class during lessons with a ruler in her hand. If anyone wasn't concentrating or not working properly she would tap the ruler on top of the desk. Years later when I was a caretaker at the local school, the head teacher came back from a school meeting and the teachers were told not to smack or touch a child's hand if they were naughty. I wonder if that was where discipline all went wrong as it seems to be now. In my generation I think we were disciplined from the word go. This is only my opinion.

A very sad day for the country and Commonwealth was when the news broke that King George VI had passed away in 1952. He had reigned for about 15 years before he became ill. Princess Elizabeth would become queen. The Princess and her husband were in Kenya at the time of her father's death but were notified immediately. The Queen Mother, as she became known, and the then Prime Minister Winston Churchill were at the airport to meet them. The queen was crowned in Westminster Abbey on the June the 2nd 1953. She looked absolutely stunning in her most beautiful dress with her six bridesmaids. I remember it so well. I was working for Mr and Mrs Balfour at the time. Televisions were just being made in black and white. There was no colour. Mr Balfour bought one and invited all the staff in to watch it. It was a very memorable day and one I will never forget. She was a very young queen when she came to the throne but what a wonderful job she did working very hard all through her reign.

10. My Falls

17 years ago I fell and shattered my elbow. I had to stay in hospital for a week. But I had a much worse fall later.

August was an extremely hot month in 2022 with pots of lovely green vegetable in the back garden it was so too difficult to keep everything watered. The two water butts we have in the back garden were completely empty in spite of both overflowing in the winter. Like my mum before me I save every drop of water I can for the vegetables and flowers to survive.

On one particular afternoon I carried little drops of water to the vegetables and I really don't know what happened. I was happy standing on my feet one minute then lying flat on the ground the next minute with my right leg trapped underneath my left leg. I just couldn't move. My son Stephen came rushing out when he saw me on the ground. He had only a week before had an operation himself which meant he couldn’t lift. He tried to get in touch with his sister but she wasn't at home so he rushed round next door to Jenny our neighbour. When she could see I couldn't move my legs she took over and called for an ambulance. Luckily it seemed they weren't that far away.

The last thing I wanted was to go to hospital but I knew I had to go. The paramedics asked what medication I was taking and then did the usual gas and air and morphine for the pain, none of which helped.

When they tried to move my legs I remember calling out *please stop the pain,* because it was so bad. *Please stop.* Eventually they managed to get my two legs apart and strap me on the stretcher. While one paramedic drove the ambulance the other one never left my side. Jenny said she would follow the ambulance with Stephen to the John Radcliffe Hospital in Oxford. I just wanted to close my eyes and go to sleep I felt so tired.

I was put in the corridor as they were so busy but it seemed like every 5 minutes they came round to ask if I was in pain. After an hour or so I was taken to a cubicle where they tested me for COVID and blood pressure and other things. I was then taken for an X-ray where they found I had broken the bone between my hip and knee and I had also fractured my pelvis. I was then taken to the same cubicle where they kept me under observation. I was next transferred to another cubicle and after a while I was transferred to the trauma ward. My son Stephen stayed with me until 1:30 in the morning.

The next morning I remember the surgeon came to see me. He told me they had so many emergencies in but he would try and get me to the operating theatre that day if he could. Unfortunately he couldn't fit it in until the Monday afternoon.

Stephen told me two friends came to see me in hospital on the Tuesday afternoon but I cannot recall them coming in. Stephen managed to find a bus from Oxford station that fitted him very well and took him straight to the hospital. He visited me every day. The following Sunday my granddaughter and her boyfriend came to see me. It was a lovely surprise as I don't see her very often. She broke the news to me that I was being transferred to another hospital and it was miles away. She contacted Stephen who said he knew nothing about it.

Telephone calls were going back and forth we were not happy but we were told if I didn't take it, another hospital will be even further away so we had no choice. I was being moved that day. It seemed a never ending journey along a very bumpy road. I think I arrived about 5:30 pm. Everything was happening so quickly. I think I had a bowl of soup at supper time and which was 7.30pm and at 7:30 pm the changeover occurred and the night staff took over. There were three female and two male nurses all dressed in nurses uniforms. I was very impressed. When they first came in, knowing that I was new there, they introduced themselves and said that if I need anything just ring the bell. They all knew their jobs and did it well. I really really liked all of them. Nothing was too much trouble for the night nurses. My thoughts were perhaps it won't be too bad after all.

The next morning, after the night and day change over, there was a tap on the door and in came Michael. He came up to me and asked: "Are you Edna?" When I said yes, he told me he was my carer for the day and he would be back in about an hour with breakfast. He looked so smart in his blue top. Jean and Mary were also patients in the ward I was in and obviously knew him.

I am a very light sleeper at the best of times but there I found it so noisy and so hot. When Michael came back he asked if I would like to sit out for breakfast or stay in bed. I sat out. It was easy for me to move from the bed to the arm chair close by. I enjoyed hot porridge and then a slice of wholemeal toast.

Because the John Radcliffe Hospital found I had osteoporosis, which is a bone condition, I wasn't allowed to walk to the bathroom on my own for fear of falling. Later Michael came in and asked me all about myself and what had happened to me when I fell. I told him I had a screw in my leg and a fractured pelvis. He asked if I wanted anything. I was nearly at the end of a really interesting book – I love reading – so I was all right.

I was told a bowl of water would be brought in for me to wash as much as I was able to do. Anything I couldn't manage they would do for me. I was able to manage most of it and was told you did very well Michael came in to see me before he went home that night. He said he wouldn't be in again until the Thursday. I thanked him for all he had done for me. Not too bad I thought.

As with the night before the night nurses were very caring and where there if one needed them.

That morning after the night nurses had handed over to the day staff a whole group of chattering, giggling young girls came past, to be given orders for the day I suppose. They all came bursting into our ward sneezing everywhere – no tissues or handkerchiefs. I did say to one girl have you got a cold. Her reply was, "Hay fever." If any of us wanted anything they were quite abrupt and not at all caring. It seemed they were all university students. It seemed to me like they were running the hospital. Apart from the night nurses I hadn't seen anyone dressed in anything related to nurses or training nurses.

The food we had came cooked from another hospital. Sometimes if you were lucky you got a nice hot meal but at other times it was warm or barely warm. A few days later I was tested for COVID. I knew I was clear of it when I left the John Radcliffe hospital but I had also heard it was in the hospital I was transferred to. I was rushed into an isolation ward and there I stayed for 12 days until I was clear.

I was still having eight painkillers a day plus morphine in my mouth in spite of not being in pain. I questioned this several times: "Why am I having to take all this when I'm not in pain?" The answer never came because she walked out of the door. I wasn't eating very much. The only two meals I really enjoyed with liver and bacon because

I also had cabbage with it, and shepherd's pie which also had cabbage and swede. Other than that no green vegetables.

I wasn't getting any exercise which I wasn't used to and was given more and more laxatives which I definitely didn't need when I was at home. When the doctor came round to see how I was, because I wasn't eating she put me on to ASSURE drinks once a day. They seemed to work very well but I had got very low and felt like giving up.

Michael asked me all about myself one evening. I enjoyed telling him. He was so interested and told me he absolutely loved talking to the 80 plus age as they were so interesting to talk to. He said you are a different breed and you ought to write a book!

Michael had two little girls and often told the told me how worried he was about their future.

When I have been there about 3 1/2 weeks I was told I would be going to the gym. I was going on the exercise bike. Because I hadn't used my legs very much it was hard going turning the pedals around but I got to what the physios wanted in the end. For a week I went on the bike every day. One day I asked if I could go on the parallel bars to strengthen my hips and legs. Very reluctantly they gave in but for once only. From then on it was only on the bike.

One day a more mature carer came in and asked if there was anything I fancied to eat after the main meal. So my son was asked to bring in some Ryvitas, tomatoes, cheese, ham and chicken that could all be put in the fridge. One day the doctor came in and was furious when she saw I was only allowed one litre of fluid a day. This included, tea, cereal, coffee or hot chocolate, gravy, soup plus water. And I like drinking. The doctor rubbed it off the board as soon as she saw it and complained to the staff.

It was so nice to be out of the ward in the television room with other patients.

After about 4 1/2 weeks in the hospital a more mature nurse came in and said, " Edna I don't have my break with the other girls. I go out in the garden for an hour. Would you like me to take you out for an hour?" I jumped at the chance and didn't need asking twice. She told me she would be back in 5 minutes with a wheelchair. The sun was so hot but to breathe the fresh air and fill my lungs, listen to the birds singing and smell the scent of the lovely flowers was pure peace and joy. It was really lovely to talk to somebody who cared and somebody different. Abby talked about her family and asked if I would like to do it again sometime. Of course I said yes please but I never saw her again. I was so pleased I had thanked her for her kindness to me and given me my life back for at least one wonderful hour.

Andrea was another nurse who was away when I arrived at the hospital. It seemed as if Andrea and Michael were doing a lot of shift work. Michael brought an iPad in for me. I wasn't into the technology of today's world so I hadn't got a clue how to use it but I was asked the programmes I wanted to watch and it was all set up for me. It was lovely to be able to watch something and each time when they came in they would set it going again for me. It was really lovely being able to see some of my usual programmes.

Jean's daughter came across to me one afternoon. She asked how I was and asked if my son was coming in to see me. I explained my son worked and, as it was so far away from home, it really wasn't worth the hassle of the journey there and back for one hour visiting. I heard afterwards some friends wanted to come to see me but weren't allowed in.

Jean's daughter asked me what I thought of the care there. My reply was that apart from one older Irish person, Andrea and Michael that seemed to be the lot care-wise. Jean's daughter then said, "I just wanted to know how you felt as you have helped mum if she couldn't find her bell or wanted help." She then said, "I don't think they care at all, so my sister and I are seriously thinking of taking mum out of here."

I thanked her for coming over and wished them all good luck for the future several times

I asked when I would be going home. Each time I was told the care package isn't in place yet. I said, "Well I don't understand as Jenny told me it was already in place whenever I wanted." One morning I heard one staff member say Edna is bed blocking they didn't need to tell me as I knew I was but it was all out of my hands Michael came in one morning and asked if I knew when I was going home. I told him it all seemed to be taken out of my hands as the hospital said the care package wasn't in place. Jenny who works at the care home said it was all a complete muddle.

The Irish staff came to me one Sunday morning and told me she had been speaking to the head physiotherapist Nicko. He was visiting the hospital that day and if he had time he would see me and see how far I was getting on with the steps. They took me to the gym about 2:00 PM and asked if I had been on the steps. When I said, "No, I hadn't," he was furious and asked why not. My answer was because I'm always made to go on the bike. Nicko explained what I had to do. The good leg to go up the step the bad leg to come down. I mastered it quite well he thought and told me I was to go on the steps every day until I was allowed home. Try as I might to get through to the girls what Nicko had said, they wouldn't hear of it and I had to get on the bike. Who was I to argue if I was only a patient?

When I had been there for 5 1/2 weeks at the hospital I was told I will be going home on the Thursday. This news cheered me a lot as you can imagine. The next day I was told you are going home on Wednesday and being transferred to a different hospital. I asked if my son knew anything about this, but I can tell you now I will not be going to Didcot Hospital when I leave here. I will be going home. I am absolutely fed up being messed around and I've had enough. After I had had a cold baked potato for tea I was told somebody would be back later to take me to the bathroom to get washed and ready for bed but no way was I to walk on my own for fear of falling over. A person with glasses I hadn't seen before took me to the bathroom and again warned me not to walk back alone: "Ring the bell when you're ready," I was told. When I had finished and was ready to go back to the ward I rang the bell and waited and waited and waited. After ringing the bell a second time I found a stool and sat down and waited. I stamped my feet on the ground and shouted to get attention but still nobody came. After what seemed like hours a nurse came rushing in. "Oh Edna we thought you were in bed asleep," she said. By this time Andrea had come in and they walked me back to the ward. The first words I heard when I stepped inside the door from Jean and Barry was, "Are you all right Edna? You've been gone ages."

I was so cross I just couldn't answer them. I had had enough and burst into tears. The nurse who rescued me said it had to be reported. I don't know if it was or not.

In the morning Michael came in and asked, "What time are you going home today, Edna?" I told him 10:00 AM but nobody would be there as my son was working. We both begged the staff to let me to stay until my son could collect me at 2:00 PM but they wouldn't hear of it. Michael said he will be back at 10:00 AM to see me before I went, but I never saw him again

When staff brought a letter in for me to take to the doctor I asked where my medication was to take home only to be told it isn't ready, so I asked why I couldn't wait until it was. The reply was, "No we will send it home by taxi at 10:00 AM."

On the dot of 10.00 a man called and said I have come to take Edna home. He told me he was from Oxfordshire County Council and they were helping the ambulance drivers as they were so busy. Although I was really happy to be going home I just hadn't slept the night before when I was told they had forgotten all about me in the bathroom and the nurse who found me told Andrea it had to be reported. I don't know if it was or not but I doubt it.

The driver was very kind and chatted a lot telling me all the visits he had had to do that day taking children to the hospital or collecting somebody who was going home or taking children to school. It was certainly a full day for him.

It took the usual 3/4 of an hour before we reached the letter box at the top of the road. I thought, "Oh good, I am nearly home." The driver took my bags and unfastened the wheelchair as he had securely fastened it before we left the hospital. The driver asked, "Which house is yours Edna?" I replied, "The one with all the flower pots outside." The flowers were out in full bloom and looked very welcoming. The driver saw me inside the door and asked if there's anything he could do for me. I knew how busy he was going to be so I said I would be all right until the carer came. I thought it would be around 12:30 or 1:00 PM and I had arrived home at 10:45 AM. It was a very lonely wait with nobody there.

I did telephone my friend, Pat, but she couldn't come as her car was having a service. At around 12:45 a knock came on the front door and in came the lovely Anna, a very bubbly, caring ,respectful and helpful person. Anna was Polish and straight away started to get what I asked for. I was so hungry by this time with only porridge for breakfast so chicken soup and toast went down so well. Anna did so much in the one hour I was allowed.

Before Anna left she told me she had seen me before. We neither us could remember but I jokingly said, "Oh one of those *once seen never forgotten.*" She went off laughing and said she would see me next morning about 7:30 AM. I thanked her so much for all she had done and said I would look forward to her next visit.

My medication from the hospital arrived by taxi at 6:30 PM that night but it was so lovely to be home again, to look out at the blue sky and see the roses in full bloom, runner beans, so many hanging down ready to pick. It was also really nice being able to talk to Steve, my son, and see all the alterations that had been done for me. I was not able to go upstairs so I had to have a commode and hospital bed downstairs. The bed wasn't at all comfortable. Stephen made sure I was all right before he went to bed and I had a bell that I could ring. The next morning I had a lovely cup of tea when Stephen made his before going to work, making sure I was all right and asking if I was in any pain. He left for work at 5:00 AM.

At 7:30 AM a little tap came on the front door and a cheery voice called, "Good morning, Edna. How are you this morning?" As I couldn't stand for long Anna brought a bowl of water for me to have a wash and clean my teeth. I did wash myself as far as I could manage but I asked Anna if she would give my back a wash. Anna had to be careful as down my spine were sore places that were very red. She gently put some cream on to heal it.

I managed myself quite well so while I did my bit Anna busied herself in making my bed, clearing things away. When I had finished then there was a cup of tea and breakfast all in the half hour I was allowed.

I began to think about the days before I had had my fall when I was busy pottering about in the garden, pulling a few weeds up, and now I was housebound, frightened to put one foot in front of the other for fear of falling again. Anna came at lunchtime for half an hour to get me some lunch and anything else I needed. Anna was so caring and encouraging. She had remembered where she had seen me before. Soon after we had come to Didcot Stephen and I walked to the shops and because we wanted some new beds we called in at Bensons and Anna was working there. Mystery solved. Jenny next door called in every night to see if I was all right.

My one concern was still having to take so much medication. I wasn't in pain but somehow I didn't seem to be thinking straight. Jenny wasn't very happy about it either so she texted 111 for advice and the doctor said they were extremely busy but somebody would come out. The doctor arrived at 6:00 AM next morning. A little Indian doctor, and very pleasant. First he asked if I was suicidal – *definitely not* was my answer! He did the usual examination and asked to see my medication to see if I wasn't in pain and said if I wasn't in pain not to take the medication, especially the morphine. He wanted me to get in touch with my doctor to take a B12 blood test.

After a few days another carer came who was called Jackie. She was very nice and caring and busied herself like Anna had done.

When I came out of hospital it took me 4 1/2 weeks to get all the painkillers – morphine etc – out of my body before I could think straight again and that was the one thing I couldn't understand. Once my mind was working properly again something seemed to tell me to test my eyes. I tried this one day when my son was watching a programme on television – covering my left eye completely and looking at the scene. My right eye was a complete black canvas.

My son got in touch with my optician for a home visit and she came out next day she was with me for over an hour and knew there was a blockage but just couldn't find out what it was, so she referred me to the John Radcliffe Eye Hospital straight away. I had an appointment after a few days. I had an eye test, eye drops and a scan and all this went straight to the Doctor who examined it. He called in Stephen who had taken me to the hospital.

When we sat down he introduced himself and said, we now know why you cannot see out of your right eye. Would you like to see? He turned the screen so we could both see. I asked what all the red was at the bottom of my eye, a fraction away from my pupil. He told me it was a big haemorrhage and put me straight away on an eye injection to try to disperse it. The doctor told me he would do all he could for me, but as it took so long for me to find the problem – it was longer than they like – and also my age didn't help, it was difficult. After a year of injections every six to eight weeks the doctor and I discussed the situation and we both said the injections were not working.

There was no injection this time but I would have to leave it about 8 weeks and see how things were going.

In the meantime I had an appointment at the eye clinic for age-related macular degeneration at the monitoring clinic on March the 12th 2024. At least they're not giving up on me.

My friend Pat was coming to see me every week as usual and we talked about when she would be able to take me out for a coffee at Marks and Spencer's. We arranged my first visit out. We were both really excited. My son would see me to Pat's car and would see me back to the house when we were coming home. Jenny came round the evening before and I told her how much I was looking forward to going out.

Kelly the physiotherapist had changed my six weeks care from the hospital to four and a half weeks. As soon as Kelly left me she emailed Jenny to stop my care immediately. When my son came home he was furious as he was still working, leaving me at 5:00 AM and getting back at 1:30 to 2:00 PM each day. He telephoned the care home and spoke to Pat the boss. She said she would help by giving me one hour a week if I could pay for it.

This also included a little bit of domestic help if possible with Anna and Jackie. This worked out well with one of them coming between 11:30 AM or 12 noon.

I had told Jennie when she came round, the night before we were going out, that Pat and myself were going out at 9:30 AM but we would be back long before 11 for Anna. We were in the car all belted up ready to leave. Pat asked if I was comfortable. We were just about to start moving off but Pat had to stop for a car coming round the corner. It turned out to be Anna. I asked her why she was so early at 9:30 AM instead of two hours later. She told me Jenny had put the time on her phone. Anna told me she would have to go and then come back to me. When I asked where she would have to go if she left, she told me the other end of Didcot. It was really embarrassing for Pat, especially for Anna, and for all of us. I told Anna she was not leaving. She knew what to do. My son would be there if there was a problem. The care home could contact me. The next day I wrote a letter to the owner of the care home and told her exactly what had happened and that I wasn't happy about it. Unfortunately there was no communication between Jenny, the office, the owner or the carers. When I asked Anna how long she had known about the change of time she said that she didn't know until she picked up her works phone that morning.

When Jackie came the next week she told me Anna had left. I asked if it was because of the week before. She told me she didn't know. Soon after Anna left I cancelled my one hour a week from the care home. Prices were about to increase and somehow it wasn't the same without Anna. I was also very upset I hadn't said goodbye and wished her luck. As I know she wasn't happy and was applying for other jobs but not unhappy about my care.

11. My 90th Birthday and Today

My 90th birthday was about one month away and I was being asked what I was going to do to celebrate. I didn't tell anyone until I had arranged it all. Stephen took me to Route 1 Garden Centre and when he left me to look at something he wanted, I made my way to the cafe. I asked if they did afternoon teas for a group of people. They told me they hadn't done it before on any scale but they would give it a go. They gave me a date when the actual number had to be finalised.

It turned out that with some family and friends plus Anna and Jackie, there would be 18 in all. My son-in-law was going to take some photographs. It was a lovely surprise when my grandson telephoned that morning, I knew he wouldn't be coming as he was on holiday. Chris my grandson is so interesting and it's great to talk to him.

When I entered the room on that day I was overwhelmed with what they had done for me. Many varieties of sandwiches, cakes, teas, coffees etc. A good time was had by all. Stephen had a beautiful cake made for me and had also brought a card for all the garden centre and café employees to sign. Oh it was a wonderful, wonderful day and one I will remember for a long time.

Evie picked up all his best photos and made it into a little book for me to keep with the many cards, balloons and messages I had been given.

Edna and Steve on her 90th birthday

Although we haven't got a big garden we make the most of it by growing vegetables in big pots. We did well last year with purple sprouting broccoli, runner beans, cauliflower, French beans, carrots and tomatoes. It is so lovely in the summer to go and pick fresh vegetables. Stephan is getting really good now, filling all the pots with new soil each year. Both the front garden with flowers and back garden. The peas we grew last year were really very good but the second showing was not so good when the pigeons got under the net and ate them. The roses, too, look lovely in a row by the fence.

I try to do my bit to help and I suppose I plod around more than plant, but between us we get there and it is so lovely to see the runner beans popping through the soil. We don't get many little birds around – far too many cats around. It's awful to see so many baby birds killed by cats and left.

Soon after we came to Didcot all one could see on the roads were dead hedgehogs. Cars go far too fast along Sandringham Road. One day soon after we came to Didcot I saw where a hedgehog been on the lawn. I was so pleased. The next time we went to the garden centre we bought a proper hedgehog house especially designed so that no cats can get into it. We put it under the garden bench. I encouraged the hedgehog by putting tiny bits of food by the edge of the lawn across the path and left some in the bowl by the house. Next morning she'd eaten it all.

She can come and go as she pleases. She is not closed in and we've had them every year since then. They had their babies in the house and like young children learning to eat we can tell the baby is trying to feed itself: the mess all around the bowl is a giveaway.

The years seem very different to me now. We had one in the house under the bench. Another one found itself under some lovely leaves at the bottom of the of the cupboard. It stayed the winter but one day I found a cat trying to get all the food.

Great excitement one morning at the end of April beginning of May. Sun was shining. Steven was looking at something and couldn't make out what it was. There was a brown hedgehog at 10:00 in the morning not caring a hoot. Tugging away at the grass it would get a mouthful and scuttle off to the back of the garden shed. This went on for quite a while. The next day the same. Steve put a bit of hay down by the shed and we put some food down. The food all disappeared and so did a lot of the water.

She must have only just finished her nest in time for the birth.

What else could I call her when the daisies were on the lawn and it was May but Daisy May. Occasionally I know she has been around as she seemed to keep at the bottom of the garden down by Stephen's magnolia tree in her own territory.

Many years ago people used to tell me as you get older you will find the time will get much quicker. My goodness how true that statement was! I cannot seem to do nearly as much as I did the year before. I'm also finding so many changes are happening. As a young girl I knew that spring, summer, autumn and winter came in that order but for the gardeners and farmers especially it is getting very difficult with the changing seasons. This year alone many wheat crops will be completely ruined because of the unusual wet August. Many farmers are talking about not growing wheat crops next year and that will make things so much more expensive for things like cattle feed, straw bedding for the animals, flour and bread.

12. Valediction

I cannot believe that yet another nice cafe has closed in Didcot, the café Pat and I used to go to after our shopping. The staff were always helpful and respectful. The usual thing: people are making a small profit, but not enough for the men at the top. We know eventually the shop itself will close as we have also heard the toilets will be the next thing to go. We are told it is just going to be blacked out at the windows. What a waste of a lovely little shop.

Greed again.

There won't be anywhere for the elderly people to meet as we have there. We used to talk to other customers who came in. Yes, there are many other places to go, but really only for the younger generation. I find other places packed to the rafters and so noisy that I have to leave.

In the meantime, I have to concentrate on the garden, The daffodils are coming through nicely, so there will hopefully be a splash of colour. The peas, beans and other vegetables were soon have to be planted, so a busy time ahead, weather permitting. It is really good exercise for me with my son’s help now he has retired.

I will soon be having my 91st birthday and everyone who comes through the door tells me how well I look. I told them that is because I keep as active as I can, with breaks in between, of course, and many of them. But I will not give in into sitting in a chair all day doing nothing, as so many people want me to do now. I still enjoy cooking and pottering about. To me that is enjoying life.

I have now come towards the end of my life story. For anyone who reads this, please don't think I had an unhappy life. Far from it. Being brought up in the right way, being disciplined in the right way, good manners, respect and everything that goes with it. All the jobs I had until I retired at 72 years old were good, happy jobs and it was after 30 years I left Cleeve Lodge in Goring on Thames. And I still hear from my ex-boss. I have kept many good friends until they passed away.

Now I have got many new ones from Goring which I enjoy seeing. I am so lucky. One has to be born into the life I have lived. No, it wouldn't be good enough for today's people, but I wouldn't change mine for the world. I have two wonderful friends to thank for encouraging me to write my story. It has taken me time, with hospital in between, but I'm finally on my last lap.

Anna, my first carer, would love to read this, but unfortunately I have no idea where she is now. She lived with her gran in Poland when she was young and had the same start in life as I did. I miss her so much. We got on so well.

It was so nice to see Jackie, my ex-carer last week and have a catch up.

So many memories in my life. One I will never forget and will remember to this day was the lovely little brick and flint cottage I was born and brought up in.

So there we are, folks. So many people might think one couldn't live like that, but believe me, I did. And I'm proud of it.

Edna – August 2024

Printed in Great Britain
by Amazon

58530347R00067